On Your Street

BY TORA STEPHENCHEL

Are there houses
on your street?

Are there tall buildings on your street?

6

Are there stores
on your street?

Is there a school
on your street?

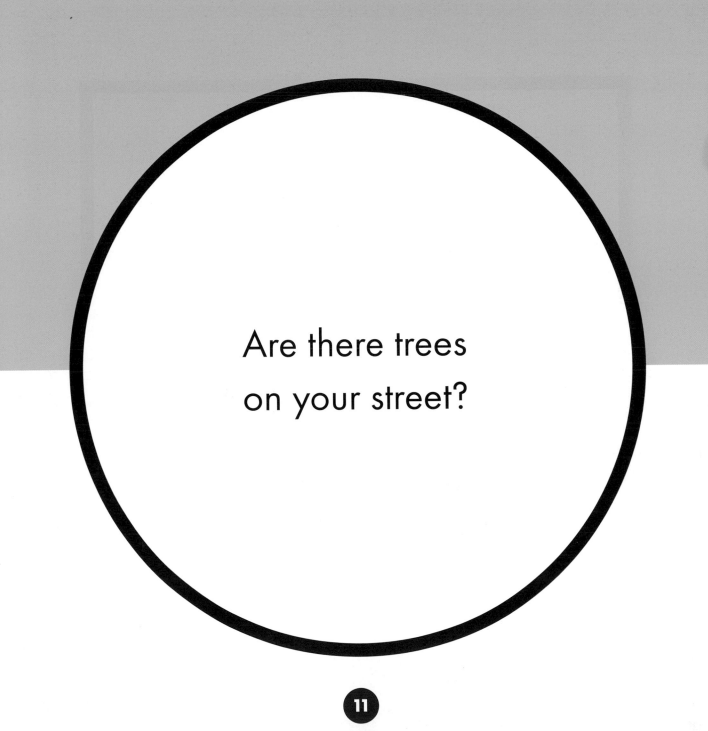

Are there trees
on your street?

Is there a park
on your street?

Are there flowers
on your street?

Is there a sidewalk
on your street?

Is there a streetlight
on your street?

There are a lot of things
on your street!

Note to Caregivers and Educators

Sight words are a foundation for reading. It's important for young readers to have sight words memorized at a glance without breaking them down into individual letter sounds. Sight words are often phonetically irregular and can't be sounded out, so readers need to memorize them. Knowing sight words allows readers to focus on more difficult words in the text. The intent of this book is to repeat specific sight words as many times as possible throughout the story. Through repetition of the words, emerging readers will recognize, and ideally memorize, each sight word. Memorizing sight words can help improve readers' literacy skills.

on

street

your

About the Author

Tora Stephenchel lives in Minnesota. She loves to spend time with her son, daughter, husband, and two silly dogs.

Published by The Child's World®
1980 Lookout Drive • Mankato, MN 56003-1705
800-599-READ • www.childsworld.com

Photographs © Albert Pego/Shutterstock.com: 6; ieronymos/Shutterstock.com: 21; Jason Finn/ Shutterstock.com: 13; littlenySTOCK/Shutterstock.com: 9; Meagan Marchant/Shutterstock.com: cover, 1; milan noga/Shutterstock.com: 18; mTaira/Shutterstock.com: 14; Richard Cavalleri/ Shutterstock.com: 2; romakoma/Shutterstock.com: 17; Sheila Fitzgerald/Shutterstock.com: 10; Sherry V Smith/Shutterstock.com: 5; Vincent Giordano Photo/Shutterstock.com: 23

ISBN 9781503845114 (Reinforced Library Binding)
ISBN 9781503846579 (Portable Document Format)
ISBN 9781503847767 (Online Multi-user eBook)
LCCN: 2020931113

Printed in the United States of America